Spiritual Enlightenment Across Traditions

Teachings from the Lineage of the Warrior, Scholar and Sage

By Jim Moltzan

Disclaimer

This book is intended for information purposes only. The author does not promise or imply any results to those using this information, nor are they responsible for any adverse results brought about by the usage of the information contained herein. Use the information provided at your own risk. Furthermore, the author does not guarantee that the holder of this information will improve his or her health from the information contained herein.

The author of this book has used his/her best efforts in preparing this book. The author makes no representation of warranties with respect to the accuracy, applicability, or completeness of the contents of this book.

This book is © copyrighted by CAD Graphics, Inc. No part of this may be copied, or changed in any form, sold, or used in any way other than what is outlined within this book under any circumstances. No part of this book may be reproduced or transferred in any form or by any means, graphic, electronic, or mechanical, including photocopying, recording, taping, or by any information storage retrieval system, without the written permission of the author.

© 2025 CAD Graphics, Inc.

ISBN: 978-1-958837-46-7

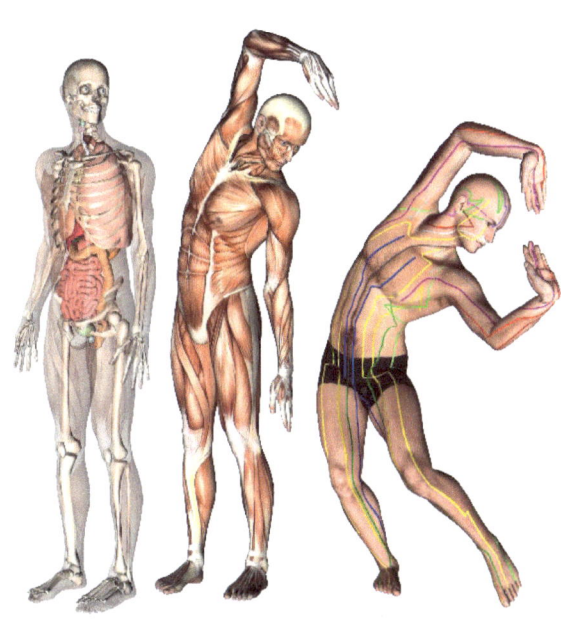

We are the architect of our own health, happiness, destiny, or fate.

Life is an echo.

What you send, comes back.

What you give, you get.

What you see in others, exists in you.

Remember, life is an echo.

It always get back to you.

So give goodness.

Table of Contents

Foreword 1
Why I Share, What I Have Learned 2
Chapter 1: Spiritual Enlightenment Across Traditions: A Comparative Analysis 3
Chapter 2: Claims, Misrepresentation, and Public Recognition 3
Chapter 3: The Challenge of Self-Proclaimed Enlightenment 3
Chapter 4: Premature and Fraudulent Claims 4
Chapter 5: Public Acknowledgment and Demonstrated Impact 4
Chapter 6: Modern Context 4
Chapter 7: Enlightenment in Buddhism 6
Chapter 8: Enlightenment in Dzogchen (Tibetan Buddhism) 7
Chapter 9: Enlightenment in Christianity 9
Chapter 10: Enlightenment in Hinduism 10
Chapter 11: Enlightenment in Judaism 12
Chapter 12: Enlightenment in Sufi Mysticism (Islamic Tradition) 12
Chapter 13: Enlightenment in Zen Buddhism 14
Chapter 14: Contemporary Spiritual Teachers on Enlightenment 15
Chapter 15: Conclusion 21

References 23

Appendices 27
    Timeline for Belief Systems 27
    Ancient Paths, Modern Peace: The Many Names of Enlightenment 29
    Chamsa Meditation 31
    About the Instructor, Author & Artist - Jim Moltzan 38
    Books Available Through Amazon 40
    Other Products 42
    Contacts 43

Foreword

In a world where the word *enlightenment* is as casually spoken as it is misunderstood, this book arrives as a timely guide and a much-needed compass. I bring over four decades of lived experience in holistic health, martial arts, and spiritual philosophy. My work has bridged continents, traditions, and generations. This is not theory woven from secondhand sources. It is a tapestry stitched from personal practice, deep study, and observation across multiple cultures and lineages.

Spiritual Enlightenment Across Traditions does not shy away from complexity. It explores the luminous heights and the shadowed pitfalls of the quest for awakening. The text honors the wisdom of ancient paths, from Buddhism's Middle Way to the contemplative traditions of Christianity, from the heart of Sufism to the Advaita vision of non-duality, while also holding space for contemporary teachers, neuroscientific insights, and the evolving language of inner transformation.

What sets this work apart is its honesty. Enlightenment here is not romanticized as a quick fix, nor confined to the rarefied realms of monastic life. It is examined in its human dimension: the signs of authenticity, the role of community and lineage, the dangers of false claims, and the subtle interplay between awakening and everyday living. In the pages ahead, the reader will find not only the luminous examples of the Buddha, Jesus Christ, the Dalai Lama, and other spiritual exemplars, but also an unflinching look at the challenges of discernment in an age of instant gurus and self-proclaimed masters.

For the serious seeker, this book is both mirror and map. It reflects the inner work needed for genuine transformation and offers a panoramic view of how different cultures and eras have understood the same eternal truth: that awakening is not an escape from life, but a deep engagement with it, while rooted in clarity, compassion, and integrity.

Whether you are stepping onto the path for the first time or refining decades of practice, may these pages serve as a companion, a provocation, and a source of steady guidance on your own journey toward the light within.

Welcome to the Path.

— Jim Moltzan

Why I Share, What I Have Learned

I made my commitment many years ago to learn, study, practice and teach fitness and well-being. My education came from martial arts and various other Eastern methods rooted in Traditional Chinese Medicine (TCM). I started when I was 16 years old and have never stopped since; 61 now.

I have written journals, produced educational graphics and co-authored a book in addition to many that I have self-authored. I blog often with a WordPress site, writing about the anatomical, physiological and mental benefits of mind and body training. Years back I started recording my classes and lectures, knowing that somewhere down the line, all of this information would be valuable to those who need and desire it.

My YouTube channel has almost 300 videos of FREE classes and other education videos. The goal all along has been to raise the awareness that Tai chi (a martial art), qigong (yoga at its root) and many other Eastern wellness methods, have proven the test of time for maintaining well-being. No gym, no mat, no membership, no special clothes or equipment. Just the individual and their engagement.

Weak or injured knees, back issues (strains & sciatica), stress & anxiety, asthma, arthritis, balance, poor posture - the list is endless. These are all issues that can be improved or overcome by those serious about learning about the mind, body & spirit connection.

Chapter 1: Spiritual Enlightenment Across Traditions: A Comparative Analysis

Spiritual enlightenment is a transformative realization of ultimate reality or truth that is revered across many of the world's religious and mystical traditions. Often described as *awakening* or *liberation*, enlightenment involves a profound shift in consciousness that frees one from ignorance, suffering, and the illusion of a separate self. Each tradition conceptualizes this highest spiritual attainment in its own terms, such as **nirvāṇa** in Buddhism, **moksha** in Hinduism, **satori** in Zen, the recognition of the **natural state** in Dzogchen, **fanā'** in Sufi Islam, and various descriptions by contemporary teachers. Yet all point to an elevated state of awareness and peace beyond ordinary perception. Despite differences in doctrine and language, these traditions share common themes of transcending the ego, attaining inner stillness or unity, and living in accordance with ultimate truth. This report provides a detailed academic overview of spiritual enlightenment as understood in:

- **Buddhism**
- **Christianity**
- **Dzogchen** (Tibetan Buddhism)
- **Hinduism**
- **Judaism**
- **Sufi mysticism**
- **Zen Buddhism**
- **contemporary spiritual teachers**

Drawing on scholarly sources and documented spiritual biographies to illuminate both the distinct and overlapping features of enlightenment across these diverse contexts.

Chapter 2: Claims, Misrepresentation, and Public Recognition

Determining whether an individual has attained spiritual enlightenment has been a point of debate across cultures and traditions. While many spiritual systems emphasize direct experience and personal realization (Kapleau, 1989), the recognition of such a state often involves more than self-proclamation. In Buddhist contexts, for example, enlightenment (*bodhi*) is traditionally confirmed by a teacher who has themselves been recognized within a lineage (Gethin, 1998). Similarly, in Advaita Vedānta, the authority of a guru, along with the disciple's demonstrable equanimity and detachment, serves as a safeguard against unfounded claims (Deutsch, 1969; Radhakrishnan, 1953).

Chapter 3: The Challenge of Self-Proclaimed Enlightenment

A significant challenge arises when individuals claim enlightenment without external verification. In the modern era, where personal narratives are easily disseminated through books, lectures, and online platforms, self-reported awakening experiences, particularly from young claimants, may gain attention without undergoing rigorous scrutiny (Taylor, 2017). Historical traditions have generally discouraged premature declarations, noting that spiritual maturity often develops over decades of disciplined practice (Easwaran, 2007). Without such maturation, profound mystical or peak experiences can be mistaken for final realization (Katz, 1984).

Chapter 4: Premature and Fraudulent Claims

Youthful claims, such as those made in the teen years, pose particular concerns. While some traditions acknowledge the possibility of early awakening, these cases are exceedingly rare and usually validated by community consensus or sustained demonstration of insight and compassion over time (Dalai Lama, 2005). Conversely, individuals motivated by status, influence, or financial gain have historically exploited spiritual language to claim exalted states, often without the behavioral consistency such realization is said to require (Schimmel, 1975). This has led to movements or followings that, upon later examination, revealed the absence of genuine transformation.

Chapter 5: Public Acknowledgment and Demonstrated Impact

Across traditions, the ultimate test of enlightenment is not merely internal conviction but observable benefit to others. In Zen Buddhism, this is expressed as "returning to the marketplace" to assist all beings (Kapleau, 1989). In Hinduism, enlightened teachers are expected to embody *lokasangraha*, or actions for the welfare of the world (Radhakrishnan, 1953). When claims lack corresponding action or positive influence, public recognition tends to be limited. Conversely, figures whose presence and conduct profoundly shift the lives of those around them often gain acknowledgment beyond their immediate circles, sometimes even entering historical record (Smith, 1999).

Chapter 6: Modern Context

1. Who Determines Enlightenment?
   a. Self-Recognition
   - **Inward Certainty** – Many spiritual traditions say enlightenment is ultimately known only by the person experiencing it, because it's an internal shift beyond conventional proof.
   - **Danger** – This makes it easy for self-delusion or ego inflation to masquerade as awakening.

   b. Teacher or Lineage Confirmation
   - **Zen & Vajrayana Buddhism** – A master may formally "certify" a student's realization after rigorous testing (e.g., *koan* practice, extended retreats, unpredictable challenges to reveal emotional stability).

- **Advaita Vedanta** – A guru might acknowledge the disciple as *jivanmukta* (liberated while living) if their behavior, clarity, and compassion demonstrate the qualities of realization.
- **Benefit** – A lineage acts as a safeguard against premature claims, assuming the lineage itself is healthy and ethical.

c. Community Recognition
- **Sangha or Faith Community** – Over time, peers and disciples may recognize someone's wisdom, humility, and the transformative impact they have on others.
- **Historical Examples** – Figures like the Buddha, St. Francis, or Ramana Maharshi were widely regarded as enlightened because of the sustained influence of their teachings and their personal conduct.

d. Historical Endorsement
- Over decades or centuries, the authenticity of a person's awakening is often judged by the **lasting value of their teachings**, the consistency of their life story, and the absence of scandals or contradictions.
- **Example** – Milarepa's story was preserved in Tibetan tradition not because he declared himself enlightened, but because his life and poetry continued to inspire for generations.

2. What Prevents or Allows False Claims?
Checks and Balances
- **Rigorous Training** – Genuine traditions put seekers through years (sometimes decades) of discipline, humility, and testing before recognition.
- **Behavioral Markers** – True awakening is said to diminish ego, greed, and attachment, while increasing compassion, patience, and service.

Risks of False Claims
- **Ego and Power** – A person can claim awakening to gain followers, money, or influence.
- **Cultural Blind Spots** – In societies that romanticize "spiritual gurus," people may not critically examine such claims.
- **Isolation** – Without a trusted community or mentor, there's no one to challenge inflated self-perceptions.
- **Misinterpretation of Experiences** – Powerful meditative or mystical states (*samadhi*, kundalini surges, psychedelic visions) can be mistaken for full awakening, though many traditions say they're only temporary milestones.

3. Red Flags in Self-Proclaimed "Enlightened" Figures

- Demands unquestioning loyalty or large sums of money.
- Claims to be the *only* true teacher or the final authority.
- Uses charisma to avoid accountability for personal behavior.
- Lacks transparency in finances, relationships, or past history.
- Has followers who become dependent rather than empowered.

4. Bottom Line
- In **healthy traditions**, enlightenment recognition is a blend of self-realization, peer/teacher verification, and observable transformation over time.
- In **unhealthy settings**, the absence of accountability makes it easy for charismatic figures to misuse the label.

In contemporary times, public scrutiny is both more immediate and more fragmented. While modern neuroscience has begun examining patterns in the brains of long-term meditators (Martin, 2010), scientific recognition does not equate to traditional validation. The interplay between ancient frameworks of discernment and modern modes of self-presentation creates both opportunities for genuine teachers to reach wider audiences and challenges in discerning authenticity (Taylor, 2017).

Chapter 7: Enlightenment in Buddhism

In Buddhism, enlightenment is most commonly referred to as *bodhi* (Sanskrit for "awakening") or **nirvāṇa**. Attaining enlightenment was the paramount goal taught by Siddhartha Gautama, the historical Buddha, who is said to have achieved full awakening under the Bodhi Tree, thereby becoming "the Buddha" (literally "the Awakened One")[1][2]. The title "Buddha" denotes one who has *awakened* from the sleep of ignorance by discovering the path to nirvāṇa, or the complete cessation of suffering, and who teaches that path to others (Siderits, 2023).

Nirvāṇa in Theravāda Buddhist doctrine is the ultimate spiritual goal defined as the extinction of **dukkha**, or suffering. It is described as the "unconditioned" state beyond birth and death, in which the causes of suffering have been eliminated (Harvey, 2013). Peter Harvey (2013) explains that nirvāṇa is the *"cessation of the painful"*, a liberation from the endless cycle of rebirth (*saṃsāra*) achieved by eradicating craving and ignorance[3][4]. The word nirvāṇa literally means "blowing out" or "quenching," as in extinguishing a fire, namely the "fires" of attachment, aversion, and delusion that fuel suffering[5][6]. When these defilements are utterly destroyed in an arahant (enlightened person), suffering ends and no further rebirth occurs[7]. Thus, in early Buddhism *bodhi* (enlightenment) is essentially synonymous with nirvāṇa, where there is a state of freedom from greed, hatred, and delusion that brings irreversible peace[8].

In the Mahāyāna Buddhist traditions, the concept of enlightenment expands to *samyak-saṁbodhi* or full Buddhahood, an omniscient liberation attained for the benefit of all beings. Mahāyāna emphasizes the "bodhisattva ideal," wherein an enlightened being forgoes final nirvāṇa to compassionately assist others. Enlightenment in Mahāyāna is often associated with realizing **śūnyatā** (emptiness) and the inherent *Buddha-nature* of all beings (Williams, 2008). It is said to involve insight into the non-duality of saṃsāra and nirvāṇa, seeing that the world of change and an enlightened reality are not two separate realms (Sebastian, 2016). In Zen (a school of Mahāyāna) and Vajrayāna contexts, enlightenment may be depicted as an immediate recognition of mind's true nature; however, these are consistent with the broader Buddhist understanding that enlightenment entails a radical transformation of perspective in which the illusion of an independent self is overcome (Gethin, 1998). All Buddhist schools hold that the enlightened individual is characterized by wisdom (*prajñā*) and compassion, having directly understood the truth of non-self (*anātman*) and impermanence, and thus is freed from attachment and suffering (Rahula, 1959).

A contemporary figure whose approach to enlightenment has extended beyond traditional validation is the 14th *Dalai Lama*. Not only regarded in Tibetan Buddhism as a living Bodhisattva, but he also actively engages with science. The Dalai Lama famously stating that Buddhism must adjust when scientific evidence contradicts its teachings (Dalai Lama, 2005). In his book *The Universe in a Single Atom* (2005), he elaborates on the convergence of phenomenological and scientific approaches to reality. His presence at neuroscience symposia and dialogues such as the Mind and Life initiative underscores a rare instance where modern spiritual leadership and empirical inquiry are directly entwined (PBS, 2005; *Wired*, 2006).

In summary, Buddhist enlightenment (nirvāṇa/bodhi) is a state of awakening to the true nature of reality, marked by the extinguishing of craving and ignorance. It is the realization of cessation, the end of suffering and rebirth, resulting in profound inner peace and liberation (Harvey, 2013). The Buddha's own enlightenment underpins this ideal: through meditative insight and moral cultivation he attained *"the state of enlightenment (bodhi) which represents the cessation of all further suffering"*[9], and spent the rest of his life teaching others the Middle Way toward that same awakening (Siderits, 2023).

Chapter 8: Enlightenment in Dzogchen (Tibetan Buddhism)

Dzogchen, often translated as "The Great Perfection," is a tradition within Tibetan Buddhism (especially the *Nyingma* school) that presents a distinctive view of enlightenment. In Dzogchen, enlightenment is understood as the direct recognition of the primordial nature of mind, which is already pure, complete, and ever-present. Unlike some paths that frame enlightenment as a goal to be achieved in the future, Dzogchen emphasizes that one's true nature is already enlightened. The task is simply to awaken to or recognize that inherent *"natural state"*. This natural state of the mind is described as a condition of *rigpa* (Tibetan: *knowledge* or *gnostic awareness*): a clear, luminous awareness untarnished by conceptual obscurations.

Dzogchen teachings maintain that nothing needs to be added or removed from the mind to attain enlightenment. The mind's essence is *originally empty* (void of ego or inherent self), yet *luminosely cognizant*. Enlightenment, then, is ever-present and *"supposed to transcend teaching and attainment"*, because from the ultimate standpoint, there is no *attaining* some new state. One simply realizes what *already is* (Boyce, 2006). As Buddhist scholar-practitioner Barry Boyce (2006) explains, *"Dzogchen's adherents claim there is no higher teaching or attainment in the Buddhist firmament. In fact, Dzogchen is supposed to transcend teaching and attainment. Its poetry and realization songs repeatedly stress the folly of trying to learn something, to gain anything, or to get anywhere at all."* Since the attempt to fabricate or chase enlightenment only reinforces the false notion that it is absent[14][15]. The paradox in Dzogchen is that while in principle everyone is already inherently enlightened (as the nature of their mind), in practice most people fail to recognize this due to ignorance (*marigpa*). The role of Dzogchen practice is to cut through that ignorance and directly point the student to the radiant emptiness of their own mind.

Practically, Dzogchen involves special meditative approaches often classified into *trekchö* (cutting through solidity to recognize the empty nature of phenomena and mind) and *thögal* (leaping over, practices that utilize vision and energy to experientially realize the *rainbow body* or the mind's luminosity). A *qualified master* is considered essential in Dzogchen, to give "pointing-out instructions" that can catalyze the student's recognition of rigpa. Indeed, Dzogchen heavily emphasizes the student-teacher relationship: *"this path does not work unless one puts all one's faith in a teacher and a lineage of teachers. There is no Dzogchen in the abstract. There is only Dzogchen as embodied in people"* (Boyce, 2006)[16]. The direct transmission from teacher to student serves to introduce the student to the nature of their own mind beyond conceptual understanding.

In describing enlightenment, Dzogchen texts often use poetic and expansive language. They liken the enlightened mind to the sky. Vast, clear, boundless and awareness to the sun that, though temporarily obscured by clouds (thoughts, emotions), always shines brilliantly. An oft-cited metaphor is that our true nature is like a mirror: *perfectly pure and able to reflect anything without being affected*. When one recognizes this "mind-as-it-is," all perceptions and thoughts are seen as spontaneous expressions (*rolpa*) of the primordial purity. The enlightened Dzogchen practitioner thus experiences reality as a spontaneous, *"effortless perfection"* where everything arises and is understood to be of one taste with emptiness and luminosity.

Comparatively, Dzogchen's view of enlightenment shares similarities with Zen and Mahāmudrā (another Tibetan meditative system). Practitioners note that the flavor of ultimate realization in various Buddhist traditions is the same, even if described differently. For instance, Dzogchen's *rigpa* can be paralleled to Zen's *kenshō* (seeing one's true nature), and its emphasis that nothing is achieved echoes Zen's teaching that there is "nothing to attain" (as the Heart Sutra states). In fact, Dzogchen masters sometimes point out that seeking enlightenment can become a hindrance; enlightenment is not a future event but the recognition of timeless awareness of the here and now. One Dzogchen saying asserts: *"Thinking of the past, one is distracted. Thinking of the future, one is deluded. Seeing the present moment, one sees that the moment is nothing (empty). If you see that moment, you see the Dharmakāya"* (the enlightened essence). This encapsulates the Dzogchen ideal of remaining in the present, in the natural state of mind, which is itself enlightenment.

Historically, Dzogchen masters like Garab Dorje, Padmasambhava, and more recently Mipham or Namkhai Norbu, have exemplified the enlightened state as one of spontaneous compassion and fearlessness arising from the recognition of mind's nature. Stories of great Dzogchen practitioners describe feats like attaining the "rainbow body" (a sign of complete realization where the physical body dissolves into light at death), emphasizing the extraordinary spiritual attainment in this path. But the teachings also stress the *ordinariness* of enlightenment: Chögyal Namkhai Norbu said, *"Dzogchen is not about going to heaven or some higher realm, it's about understanding the condition of our everyday life, here and now"*. Similarly, Chögyam Trungpa Rinpoche noted that true realization in Dzogchen is marked by profound humility and groundedness: *"Dzogchen is the place where we finally, thankfully, get off the high horse of our spirituality and just plain be"* (quoted in Boyce, 2006)[17]. In other words, an enlightened Dzogchen adept is simply *fully human*, free of pretense and dualistic struggle, spontaneously ethical and compassionate because they see no separation between themselves and others.

In conclusion, Dzogchen enlightenment is the recognition of *"mind's innate purity and perfection"* (often termed the Nature of Mind). It is a state of unwavering, present awareness (*rigpa*) in which all phenomena are experienced as inseparable from the empty cognizance of one's own mind. This Great Perfection is considered the highest teaching in Tibetan Buddhism's Nyingma lineage, a direct path to awakening that, when realized, reveals that one has *always* been Buddha, from the very beginning (Boyce, 2006).

Chapter 9: Enlightenment in Christianity

Christianity approaches enlightenment primarily through the lens of *theosis*, a Greek term meaning "divinization" or "union with God" and divine illumination through the Holy Spirit. This state is not self-realized but is understood as the believer being transformed "from glory to glory" (*2 Corinthians 3:18*, New International Version, 2011) into the likeness of Christ.

Jesus Christ as the Model of Enlightenment

Jesus Christ embodies perfect communion with God. His affirmation, *"Whoever has seen me has seen the Father"* (John 14:9, NIV, 2011), positions Him as the definitive human expression of divine presence (McGinn, 2006).

Mystical Theology and the Path to Union

Prominent Christian mystics have mapped this journey:

- **St. Teresa of Ávila** described a soul's progression through successive "mansions" toward *spiritual marriage* with Christ (Underhill, 2002).

- **St. John of the Cross** elaborated how purification through the *"dark night of the soul"* readies the believer for union with God (McGinn, 2006).

- **Meister Eckhart** taught about the "birth of God in the soul," stirring controversy and prompting scrutiny by church authorities (McGinn, 2006).

Practices that Foster Illumination

Transformative spiritual disciplines include:

- **Contemplative prayer**, where one rests silently in God's presence (Thomas Merton's tradition; see Merton, 2003).
- **Lectio divina**, a devotional reading method moving from scripture to direct communion (Underhill, 2002).
- **Fasting and asceticism**, enabling focused spiritual openness (McGinn, 2006).
- **Sacramental life**, where grace is encountered through rites like Eucharist and Baptism (McGinn, 2006).

Recognition of the Enlightened

Enlightened Christians may be affirmed through canonization, public veneration, or the longevity of their spiritual legacy. St. Francis of Assisi, for instance, radiated Christ-like humility and compassion (McGinn, 2006).

Institutional Tensions

Mystical expression often found itself at odds with ecclesiastical structures. The Beguine mystic Marguerite Porete was executed in 1310 for her book *The Mirror of Simple Souls*, which described a soul's annihilation in God, an expression deemed heretical (McGinn, 2006).

Modern Expressions

Contemporary movements like *Centering Prayer* revived contemplative practice for laypeople (Keating, 1991). These forms of Christian spirituality allow for contemplative depth beyond monastic confines and foster dialogue with other traditions exploring union and presence (McGinn, 2006).

Chapter 10: Enlightenment in Hinduism

In the Hindu tradition, the equivalent of enlightenment is commonly known as ***moksha*** (Sanskrit for "liberation"), the release from the cycle of rebirth (*saṃsāra*) and union with ultimate reality. Within the philosophical schools of Hinduism (especially Vedānta), enlightenment is understood as realizing the true nature of the *Self* (ātman) and its unity with *Brahman*, the absolute cosmic principle. In Advaita Vedānta (a non-dual school), this realization is expressed in the Upanishadic dictum *"tat tvam asi"* ("That art Thou"), meaning one's individual consciousness is ultimately identical with Brahman. Attaining moksha thus means overcoming the illusion of separateness and knowing one's Self as the infinite, immortal reality (Deutsch, 1969).

Hindus generally see life as governed by *karma* and *saṃsāra*, an unending cycle of births and deaths. The problem is that the soul remains bound in this cycle due to ignorance *(avidyā)* of its true divine nature. The solution, as described in Hindu philosophy, is *"emancipation (moksha) from this morass … an escape from the impermanence that is inherent in mundane existence"* (Dimock & van Buitenen, 2025). In other words, enlightenment is the *eternal* and *unchanging* state beyond the transient world, it is realizing "the one permanent and eternal principle: the One, God, Brahman" and recognizing that *one's very being is identical with Brahman* (Dimock & van Buitenen, 2025). Those who have not realized this identity are considered deluded by *Maya* (illusion), whereas the enlightened sage directly experiences the truth that the individual Self (*ātman*) and the universal Brahman are one[10][11]. This knowledge *(jñāna)* dispels spiritual ignorance, bringing freedom from the cycle of karma.

Classical Hindu texts describe multiple yogic paths to attain this enlightenment. The *Bhagavad Gītā*, for example, outlines three primary margas (paths) toward moksha:

> ***jñāna-marga*** (the path of knowledge and philosophical inquiry)
>
> **bhakti-marga** (the path of devotion and love for God)
>
> **karma-marga** (the path of selfless action)[12].

All these paths aim at purification of the mind and the removal of egoistic attachments so that the seeker can perceive the ātman-Brahman unity. The Upanishads, foundational mystical scriptures of Hinduism, declare that the inner Self of a person (*ātman*) is one with Brahman, the underlying reality of the cosmos. Enlightenment is experiencing that *"the Self is Brahman"* with total certainty (Radhakrishnan, 1953). In the state of moksha, a person achieves absolute peace, bliss (*ānanda*), and freedom, often described as being like a drop merging back into the ocean. When the enlightened soul is freed from the body at death, it does not take birth again but "returns to Brahman, like a drop of water returning to the ocean" (Upanishads, as paraphrased by Easwaran, 2007).

It should be noted that different Hindu traditions have nuanced interpretations of enlightenment. *Advaita Vedānta* emphasizes a *sudden insight* into non-duality, or the eradication of ignorance through discriminative knowledge, as exemplified by teachings of Śaṅkara. In contrast, Yoga school (as in Patanjali's *Yoga Sūtras*) describes enlightenment (kaivalya) as the culmination of meditative practice, where the Seer abides in its pure nature, separate from the turbulence of the mind. Devotional traditions (like *Vaishnavism*) frame the highest goal as loving union with a personal God (e.g., Krishna), sometimes called *sayujya* or *samādhi* in God's presence, which is akin to enlightenment through grace. Despite these varied approaches, the common thread in Hindu thought is that enlightenment entails self-realization, where there is a direct, experiential knowing of the soul's eternal reality. It is liberation from ego and rebirth, marked by the insight that the deepest Self and the ultimate divine reality are fundamentally one (Dimock & van Buitenen, 2025). The enlightened being *(Jīvanmukta)* is said to be filled with equanimity, no longer driven by worldly desires, seeing the Self in all beings and all beings in the Self (Bhagavad Gītā VI.29). This state of spiritual freedom is considered the highest attainment in Hindu philosophy, equivalent to immortality in consciousness and unshakeable bliss.

Chapter 11: Enlightenment in Judaism

In Judaism, the idea of "enlightenment" is expressed through concepts such as divine illumination, prophetic insight, and mystical union with God. While the Hebrew Bible depicts Moses as speaking "face to face" with God (Exod. 33:11), later Jewish mysticism, especially the *Kabbalah,* frames enlightenment as attaining *devekut* (cleaving to God) through disciplined study, prayer, and contemplation. Figures such as Rabbi Akiva (c. 50–135 CE) and Isaac Luria (1534–1572) are often cited as paragons of Jewish mystical attainment (Scholem, 1995). Methods include rigorous *Torah* and *Talmud* study, the meditative practice of *hitbodedut* taught by Rebbe Nachman of Breslov (1772–1810), and Kabbalistic visualization of divine emanations (*sefirot*). Public acknowledgment in Jewish tradition often comes via rabbinic authority or spiritual leadership, though false messianic movements such as that of Sabbatai Zevi in the 17th century. These illustrate the tension between genuine mystical experience and questionable claims (Idel, 2005).

Chapter 12: Enlightenment in Sufi Mysticism (Islamic Tradition)

The Prophet Muhammad's mystical mi'raj (Night Journey) is often interpreted as a paradigm of ultimate spiritual ascent (Nasr, 2009). In **Sufi mysticism** the esoteric, contemplative dimension of Islam, or the concept analogous to enlightenment is often described in terms of *fanā'* and *baqā'*. *Fanā'* literally means "annihilation" or "passing away," and refers to the dissolution of the individual ego-self in the experience of the Divine. *Baqā'* means "subsistence" or "continuance," and refers to what comes after fanā': the mystic's enduring life *in and with God.* Together, fanā' and baqā' signify the apex of the Sufi spiritual journey. A transformative union with God in which the self is utterly effaced in God's presence, then "reborn" or sustained by God's eternal reality (Böwering, 2016). Gerhard Böwering (2016) defines this dual notion as *"passing away from worldly reality and being made subsistent in divine reality,"* describing the culmination of mystical experience and union with God. In other words, the enlightened Sufi is one who has "passed away" from their limited, worldly identity and lives on in a state of abiding communion with the Divine[18][19].

A Sufi seeker (*salik*) typically travels through various spiritual "stations" (*maqāmāt*) and "states" (*ahwāl*) through prayer, asceticism, and most importantly love and remembrance of God (*dhikr*). Enlightenment in Sufism is not conceptualized as *knowledge* in an abstract sense but as gnosis (*ma'rifa*), a deep, intimate knowing of God obtained by purifying the heart. The process is often described using the language of love: the seeker is the lover (*'āshiq*) and God is the Beloved (*ma'shuq*); the ultimate goal is to *"die to oneself"* in the fire of love and live only in God. When a Sufi attains *fanā' al-nafs* (annihilation of the ego), they experience the reality of *tawḥīd*, that *"there is nothing but God."* In this state, all that exists is seen as a manifestation of God, and the independent self is recognized as an illusion. Classic Sufi authors describe it as *"the drop becomes one with the ocean, "* where the individual soul (drop) loses its separateness in the ocean of divine Being. Importantly, as Böwering (2016) notes, this is not a nihilistic nothingness: *"though possibly similar in meaning to the Buddhist nirvāṇa, fanā' does not denote the extinction of individual life"*[20]. Instead, the person's false self (the ego with its egotism and passions) is extinguished, making way for the true Self to "subsist" in God (baqā')[21][22]. In the words of renowned Sufi master Abu Yazid al-Bistami, *"to know God, one must become God,"* is an expression of the idea that the self must vanish to leave only the Divine reality (Smith, 1999).

The experience of Sufi enlightenment is often ecstatic and ineffable. Many Sufi mystics have resorted to poetry to hint at its nature. For example, the 13th-century Persian poet Jalāl ad-Dīn Rūmī, who describes the merging of lover and Beloved: *"I, you, he, she, we – in the garden of mystic lovers, these are not true distinctions."* Another famous Sufi, Mansur al-Hallāj, is remembered for his ecstatic utterance *"Ana al-Ḥaqq"* ("I am the Truth [God]"). In that moment of fanā', al-Hallāj perceived no separation between himself and al-Ḥaqq (a name of God meaning *The Real* or *Truth*), effectively saying he was one with God, a statement that cost him his life, as it was deemed heretical by the orthodox. His statement, however, is often interpreted by Sufis not as blasphemy but as the cry of a lover lost in union, having obliterated the self so that only God remained speaking through him.

Sufi manuals and treatises articulate the stages of this journey. Al-Junayd of Baghdad (10th century), a pivotal early Sufi, explained fanā' as the "passing away of the attributes of the self, and baqā' as the permanence of the attributes of God in the self." That is, as the ego's qualities (pride, selfish desire, etc.) fade, they are replaced by qualities of God (compassion, generosity, wisdom), which then shine through the enlightened person (Schimmel, 1975). In this sense, the enlightened Sufi does not vanish into inactivity; rather, they return from the peak of mystical union with a transformed consciousness. This is often likened to a sobering up after the "drunkenness" of the ecstatic union. While in the height of fanā' the mystic may appear utterly lost in God (even unconscious of the world), in baqā' they come back to functional existence *within* the world but remain inwardly united with God. The Persian Sufi Hafez alludes to this when he says: *"From the drunkards learn the way to the tavern, but the one who reaches the tavern returns sober"*. The notion is that a true knower of God ultimately returns to society, "sober" but carrying the fragrance of the divine.

In terms of behavior and mindset, an enlightened Sufi (often called "walī" or friend of God, also translated as saint) is characterized by complete humility, compassion, and unwavering faith. They have no will or goal apart from God's will. In the words of the 11th-century Sufi Ali Hujwiri, *"The saint's will is God's will, for he has no existence left in himself. He is like a tool in the hands of God."* Such a person is said to live in constant *dhikr* (remembrance of God), even as they perform ordinary tasks. They perceive God's presence everywhere and in all people; thus they are often filled with profound love for creation.

It is noteworthy that Sufi enlightenment experiences have been compared cross-religiously. Scholars have drawn parallels between fanā' and the Buddhist Nirvana or the Hindu concept of samādhi (Böwering, 2016). However, there are differences: Sufi union remains a relationship of lover and Beloved. Even in the utmost union, many Sufis maintain a slight distinction (as in "I am God's and God is mine"), whereas Advaita Vedanta would say the soul simply *is* Brahman. Still, the late phases of Sufi realization blur any sense of duality. The Encyclopaedia Iranica notes that while fanā' resembles Nirvana in the sense of extinguishing the ego, *"the Sufi's self is not reduced to pure nothingness"* – rather it is transformed and elevated (Böwering, 2016)[23][24].

In conclusion, Sufi mysticism conceives enlightenment as a journey of love culminating in *fanā' wa baqā'* or the annihilation of the illusory self and abiding in God's eternal reality. It is a state of union wherein the Sufi realizes the Quranic truth *"verily, we belong to God and to Him do we return"* in the most immediate way. This enlightened state manifests as a life of complete devotion, egoless service, and the radiant reflection of divine qualities. As Rūmī beautifully summed up the outcome: *"The sufi is a mirror: the one not enlightened by them is not a sufi,"* meaning the enlightened Sufi becomes a clear mirror in which others may see God's light.

Chapter 13: Enlightenment in Zen Buddhism

Zen is a school of *Mahāyāna* Buddhism (particularly influential in Japan and China, where it is called *Chan*) that places central emphasis on achieving enlightenment through direct experience rather than through scriptural study or ritual. The Zen term for enlightenment is commonly **satori**, Japanese for "understanding" or "awakening"), also known as **kenshō**, or "seeing one's true nature"). Satori in Zen refers to a sudden, intuitive experience of awakening. A a profound realization of the true nature of one's mind and reality. It is often depicted as *beyond description or intellectual comprehension*, an insight that must be personally experienced. According to the *Encyclopedia Britannica*, *"Satori is said to be unexplainable, indescribable, and unintelligible by reason and logic"* – it is an inner breakthrough comparable to what Gautama Buddha experienced under the Bodhi tree (Britannica, n.d., *Satori*). In fact, Zen considers satori the very goal of its practice, a direct realization that brings about a *"complete reordering of the individual in relation to the universe"*, akin to a spiritual rebirth (Britannica, n.d., *Satori*).

Zen training is designed to precipitate such enlightenment experiences. It famously utilizes methods like *zazen* (sitting meditation) and *kōan* practice (contemplating paradoxical riddles) to exhaust the analytical mind and trigger insight. A defining theme in Zen is the tension between gradual cultivation and sudden awakening. The two major Japanese Zen branches approach this differently: the *Sōtō* school emphasizes quiet, ceaseless meditation (*shikantaza* or "just sitting") where enlightenment is seen as a gradual unfolding. Practitioners express an *"identity of practice and enlightenment,"* meaning that the very act of sitting in awareness is itself enlightenment in the present moment (Suzuki, 1970). In contrast, the *Rinzai* school places greater weight on abrupt, breakthrough experiences, employing kōans and dynamic interactions with a master to spark a dramatic satori (Suzuki, 1956). As Britannica notes, *"the Sōtō sect emphasizes quiet sitting (zazen), whereas the Rinzai sect devotes more attention to methods of bringing about an abrupt awakening"* (Britannica, n.d., *Satori*)[13]. Both schools, however, ultimately value the *insight into one's own true nature*, often phrased in Zen as "seeing into one's "original mind" or discovering that one's Buddha-nature has been present all along.

Zen literature is rich with accounts of enlightenment experiences, often spontaneous and triggered by seemingly simple events. A sudden sound, a casual word from a teacher, or even mundane tasks. These anecdotes (in Zen *mondo* or kōan collections) illustrate that enlightenment can flash forth unexpectedly when the student is properly prepared. Satori is not a permanent state at first, but an initial glimpse (*kenshō*) of reality; sustained enlightenment requires further practice to integrate that insight into one's daily life. Master Hakuin, a great 18th-century Rinzai Zen master, for example, spoke of having many satori experiences, coupled with continuous effort to purify and deepen his realization afterwards. The characteristics of Zen enlightenment include a deep sense of clarity, unity, and naturalness, often described as experiencing the "suchness" (*tathatā*) of reality without the filter of discriminative thought. A person who has attained Zen enlightenment is sometimes described as being "without ego, without delusive thought," fully present and responsive to the here and now. Zen practitioners often caution, however, against becoming attached to the idea or experience of enlightenment; the Zen path stresses a certain ordinary simplicity even after awakening. This is captured in Zen sayings like *"Before enlightenment, chop wood, carry water; after enlightenment, chop wood, carry water"*, implying that enlightened awareness is to be found in the most ordinary activities when one's mind is fully present.

In summary, Zen enlightenment (satori) is an immediate, intuitive awakening to "things as they are" in a direct insight that defies intellectual explanation but utterly transforms one's perspective. It usually comes about after long preparation through meditation and mindfulness, though the final breakthrough may be sudden (Kapleau, 1989). In satori, the false dichotomy between self and world falls away: the Zen adept feels at one with the world, experiencing reality *directly* without the mediation of conceptual thought. Zen texts often compare satori to "waking up" to a reality that was always there: as one Zen master put it, *"Enlightenment is like the moon reflected on water. The moon does not get wet, nor is the water broken."* The essential nature of reality remains as it is, but one's mind becomes clear and still enough to perfectly reflect it. Such poetic expressions underscore Zen's view that enlightenment is not a distant goal but the realization of one's ever-present original nature. The enlightened Zen practitioner, having experienced satori, continues the practice with a "beginner's mind" where engaging life with spontaneity, compassion, and a freedom from attachments, embodying wisdom in each moment.

Chapter 14: Contemporary Spiritual Teachers on Enlightenment

In the modern era, outside of formal religious institutions, a number of contemporary spiritual teachers have emerged who experienced and taught about enlightenment. These individuals often draw upon traditional insights (from Buddhism, Hinduism, etc.) but present them in a secular or interfaith language accessible to people regardless of religious background. Contemporary discussions of enlightenment frequently emphasize psychological transformation, with the transcendence of the ego, living in the present moment, and the direct experience of peace and unity. Below, I explore a few influential modern teachers and their perspectives on enlightenment, supported by well-documented accounts of their experiences.

Ramana Maharshi (1879–1950) – A revered Indian sage from Tamil Nadu is a prime example of a modern enlightened teacher in the Hindu *Advaita Vedānta* tradition. Ramana's enlightenment occurred spontaneously when he was just 16 years old. In 1896, without any formal training, Ramana had a sudden intense fear of death. Instead of panicking, he turned his attention inward to investigate the nature of dying. Lying down as if dead, he asked himself, *"Who is it that dies? What is death?"* and experienced a profound shift: *"The body dies, but I am still here, I am the deathless Spirit"* (Sivananda, n.d.). In his own recounting of that moment, Ramana said: *"The shock of the fear of death drove my mind inwards… I held* *my breath and thought, 'Well then, let this body die. What remains? What is it that is aware of this death?' All at once, I was overcome by a flood of Self-awareness – an overwhelming feeling of reality and presence. The 'I' or my true Self stood forth alone, eternal and alive, and the fear of death vanished forever"* (as quoted in Swami Sivananda's *Lives of Saints*). This death experience led to what he later described as a permanent awakening: from that day, the young Ramana lost interest in mundane life, soon left home for the sacred mountain Arunachala, and remained established in the state of pure awareness for the rest of his life[25][26].

Ramana Maharshi became known for teaching a simple yet profound method of self-inquiry (*ātma-vichāra*) to help others realize enlightenment. He instructed seekers to focus on the fundamental question *"Who am I?"* and to earnestly seek the source of the ego or the sense of individuality. According to Ramana, enlightenment is the discovery of the Self (which he equated with the infinite Brahman) as one's true identity. A discovery that reveals that the personal "I" was never anything but an illusion. He often affirmed, "Enlightenment is simply to *remain as the Self*," meaning to abide as pure awareness, free from identification with the body-mind (Maharshi, 1985). Those who sat with Ramana frequently reported experiencing a taste of deep peace or stillness in his presence. Remarkably, Ramana had no guru and minimal religious education; his case is a testament to the possibility of spontaneous enlightenment. His biography and recorded dialogues (e.g., *Talks with Sri Ramana Maharshi*) are considered classic spiritual literature. In them, Ramana describes the enlightened state as one of silent, unwavering bliss and equanimity. He lived a very simple, unassuming life, and was observed to be consistently compassionate, egoless, and immersed in a steady state of inner peace, all practical hallmarks of an enlightened being in the eyes of his devotees.

Jiddu Krishnamurti (1895–1986) provides another intriguing modern perspective. Krishnamurti was groomed in his youth by the Theosophical Society to be a world teacher, but he later rejected formal roles and religious labels, emphasizing individual freedom. In the 1920s, Krishnamurti underwent a series of mystical experiences termed "the process," involving intense pain followed by states of immense clarity and bliss (Lutyens, 1971). He described a pivotal experience in 1922 where he felt "the Presence of the Divine" and a profound unity with all existence. Following this, Krishnamurti's teaching was that truth is a pathless land. Enlightenment cannot be approached via any organized belief or path, but only through direct observation and choiceless awareness in the present. He did not use the word enlightenment frequently but essentially spoke of freedom. Freedom from the known, from conditioning, fear, and ego, as the essence of a transformed life. In Krishnamurti's view, when the mind is utterly silent and free of its self-centered activity, a qualitatively different state of consciousness (sometimes he called it *"immensity"* or *"the other"*) manifests, which could be likened to enlightenment. He famously engaged in dialogues (with scientists, Buddhist scholars, etc.) pointing to the immediate possibility of radical insight that ends sorrow and conflict. Krishnamurti's life and teachings, documented in numerous books and biographies, exemplify a non-sectarian approach to enlightenment that resonated with many secular and western audiences. He demonstrated that one could discuss enlightenment without any religious framework, focusing on psychological freedom and the awakening of intelligence and compassion in daily life.

Eckhart Tolle (b. 1948) is a contemporary spiritual teacher who has reached a global audience with his account of sudden enlightenment and its implications for personal transformation. Tolle, originally from Germany, experienced debilitating depression and anxiety in his early adulthood. One night, in 1977, at age 29, he underwent a dramatic inner crisis that became an awakening. He describes reaching a point of nearly suicidal despair when a thought struck him: *"I cannot live with myself any longer."* This triggered a spontaneous inquiry: if "I" cannot live with "myself," are there two selves? *"I felt drawn into a vortex of energy,"* he recounted, *"As if I were sinking into a void. Suddenly, there was no more fear."* Tolle awoke the next morning in a state of unprecedented peace and freedom, perceiving the world with fresh wonder (Tolle, 1999). He had undergone a shift into a state of presence, wherein compulsive thinking subsided, and a deep joy arose from simply *being*. He later realized that in that moment of surrender, his egoic mind had effectively collapsed, yielding an enlightened state of consciousness (Tolle, 1999). As Tolle describes, *"The identification with my mind, that life of incessant mental noise, suddenly stopped. I was fully conscious, but there were no more thoughts. I felt the presence of the Oneness. And then I spent the next few years sitting blissfully on park benches, watching the world go by"* (paraphrased from *The Power of Now*).

Eckhart Tolle's teachings, articulated in best-selling books like *The Power of Now* (1999) and *A New Earth* (2005), distill the essence of enlightenment in straightforward terms. He emphasizes living in the Now, since psychological time (being stuck in past regrets or future anxieties) is a primary impediment to awakening. For Tolle, enlightenment is the "end of suffering" through the dissolution of the ego (Tolle, 1999). The ego is the false self, as a mental construct of identity based on memories and projections. When one is present and no longer completely run by the ego-mind, a new dimension of consciousness emerges, inner peace, acceptance of what is, and a sense of oneness with life. Tolle often uses the term "awakening" rather than enlightenment, highlighting that it is not an abstract attainment but a shift available to anyone *here and now*. He also integrates insights from multiple traditions: for instance, he speaks of the ego in a way similar to Buddhism's notion of *dukkha* arising from attachment to a self, and echoes Advaita Vedānta by identifying our true nature as the formless awareness behind mental phenomena. Tolle's own radical transformation and his ability to communicate these ideas in secular language have made his work widely influential. Psychologists and neuroscientists have even shown interest in Tolle's accounts as an example of a possible spiritual awakening experience that brings about enduring positive change (Taylor, 2017).

Many other contemporary figures could be discussed, such as **Paramahansa Yogananda** (1893–1952), who wrote *Autobiography of a Yogi* detailing his enlightenment experiences and those of his lineage; **Sri Aurobindo** (1872–1950), a modern Indian mystic who spoke of a supramental enlightenment transforming even the physical body; **Alan Watts** (1915–1973), who interpreted Eastern enlightenment for Western audiences; **Adyashanti** (b. 1962), an American teacher whose Zen-influenced awakening led him to teach a form of "true meditation" and the discovery of one's always-enlightened nature; or **Byron Katie** (b. 1942), who, like Tolle, awakened suddenly out of depression and then taught self-inquiry (The Work) to help others shift their consciousness. Despite differences in personality and emphasis, contemporary enlightened teachers often converge on key points: that our ordinary sense of self is a kind of illusion or constriction; that it is possible to "wake up" from this condition into a more authentic, liberated state; and that this awakening is marked by inner stillness, compassion, and a recognition of interconnection or unity. They also tend to stress that enlightenment is not a cold, detached state, but rather, it releases great compassion and love, because in seeing through the ego's separateness, one identifies with all life.

Another interesting aspect of modern teachers is the demystification of enlightenment. They often refrain from exotic terminology, instead describing enlightenment in psychological or metaphorical terms. For instance, Jack Kornfield, a Buddhist teacher and psychologist, famously said: *"After the enlightenment, the laundry,"* meaning that awakening does not remove one from the tasks of human life. This aligns with the notion that enlightened individuals still face challenges and emotions but relate to them from a place of clarity and non-attachment. Modern accounts frequently highlight that enlightenment is not a fixed end point; there can be degrees of awakening and a continual deepening (Wilber, 2000). Thus, contemporary discourse sometimes uses the term "awakening" as a dynamic process rather than a one-time event.

It is also worth noting the scientific interest in enlightenment experiences in recent decades. Researchers in psychology and neuroscience have begun studying reports of sudden or gradual "quantum change" and persistent non-symbolic experience (Martin, 2010) that correspond to traditional enlightenment. While science is far from fully understanding these states, preliminary findings (using brain imaging, for example) have noted distinct patterns in long-term meditators or "enlightened" individuals, such as altered activity in brain networks related to the self (e.g., reduced default mode network activity). Such studies treat enlightenment as a human potential that can perhaps be understood in terms of consciousness and cognitive processes. Contemporary spiritual teachers sometimes engage with these perspectives, bridging ancient wisdom and modern knowledge.

In summary, contemporary spiritual teachers reaffirm the core insight of the enlightenment traditions, that human beings can undergo a profound shift of identity from the limited ego to a vast, peaceful awareness. Through their biographies and teachings, they illustrate that enlightenment is not merely a historical or monastic phenomenon but a living reality that can manifest in various cultural contexts today. Whether it's Ramana Maharshi's quiet radiance on a South Indian hillside, J. Krishnamurti's incisive dialogues dissolving psychological barriers, or Eckhart Tolle's gentle guidance into present-moment awareness, these modern exemplars demonstrate the *"perennial philosophy"* (Huxley's term) that the enlightened state, however described, is real, transformative, and accessible. Their lives also underscore that enlightenment expresses itself in compassion, simplicity, and service: Ramana's silent benevolence toward visitors and animals, Krishnamurti's insistence on total honesty and freedom, Tolle's work in helping others find peace, all suggest that genuine awakening benefits the wider world, not just the individual. In the end, contemporary teachers bring the message that enlightenment is not confined to ancient times or cloisters; it speaks to the fundamental liberation and awakening of *human consciousness*, here and now, in the midst of everyday life.

Spiritual Masters: Ages, Paths, and Aims (Chronological by Awakening Age)

Figure	Age at Awakening / Key Event	Method	Goal
Swami Brahmananda Saraswati *(Guru Dev)*	Began renunciation at ~9 years old; became disciple at 14; full sannyas at 34; Shankaracharya at 70.	Intense renunciation, solitude, discipline, and guru-guided transformation.	Realization of Advaita (non-duality), liberation, and spiritual leadership.
14th Dalai Lama (Tenzin Gyatso)	Recognized as reincarnation at ~2; enthroned at 15; deep spiritual maturation over decades.	Tibetan Buddhist study, meditation, debate, and compassion practices; active dialogue with science.	Preserve Tibetan Buddhism, embody Bodhisattva ideal, and integrate ancient wisdom with modern science.
Hakuin Ekaku *(Rinzai Zen master)*	24 years old; profound insight after 7 days in a temple shrine, triggered by a bell strike.	Rigorous Zen training, *koan* practice, meditative focus, and challenging teacher–student exchanges.	*Kensho* (initial awakening) followed by post-satori practice to deepen clarity and compassion.
Adyashanti *(American spiritual teacher)*	Transformative experiences began ~25; full realization by 31.	Meditation, contemplation, self-inquiry, and study of diverse traditions.	Realize universality—emptiness and interconnectedness—then live that realization in daily life.
Jesus Christ	Baptized around age 30; "filled with the Holy Spirit," began ministry; transfiguration as key mystical moment.	Prayer, fasting, teaching, healing, parables, and sacrifice.	Proclaim the Kingdom of God, redeem humanity, and model divine love.
Gautama Buddha	~35 years old, after years of ascetic practice and meditation under the Bodhi Tree.	Intensive meditation and renunciation, followed by insight into the Four Noble Truths and the Middle Way.	Achieve *nirvana*—liberation from suffering, samsara, and ignorance.
Prophet Muhammad	~40 years old, received first revelation in the Cave	Retreat, contemplation, receiving divine	Deliver the message of Islam—submission to God—and guide humanity toward righteousness.

Figure	Age at Awakening / Key Event	Method	Goal
	of Hira via the Angel Jibril (Gabriel).	revelation over 23 years (*Qur'an*).	
Contemporary Dzogchen Masters *(e.g., Chögyé Trichen Rinpoche)*	Said to achieve "rainbow body" at death, often after decades or lifetimes of practice.	Dzogchen meditation on the natural state of mind.	Liberation beyond the physical realm.
Ascended Masters / Mahatmas *(Theosophical tradition)*	Enlightenment achieved over many incarnations.	Mystical transformations across lifetimes.	Immortal, enlightened state, often guiding humanity.

Chapter 15: Conclusion

Across these diverse traditions of Buddhism, Hinduism, Zen, Dzogchen, Sufism, and modern teachings, spiritual enlightenment emerges as a unifying thread, described as the highest state of human spiritual development. Each tradition employs its own conceptual framework and metaphors: **cessation of suffering** and **nirvāṇa** in Buddhism, **Self-realization** and **moksha** in Hinduism, the intuitive **satori** of Zen, the inherent **Great Perfection** of Dzogchen, the **annihilation in the Divine** of Sufi fana, and the **ego-transcendence** or "awakening" described by contemporary teachers. Despite outward differences, these accounts exhibit remarkable *commonalities*. In all cases, enlightenment involves a radical shift beyond the ordinary ego-bound perception to a liberating recognition of a deeper reality, whether it be the non-self nature of phenomena, the oneness of the soul with God, or the spacious presence of pure awareness. Enlightened individuals, from the Buddha or mystics of old to present-day teachers, consistently exhibit qualities of profound inner peace, compassion, clarity, and fearlessness. They testify to the potential for human consciousness to be *transformed* – freed from ignorance, suffering, and selfishness.

However, it is equally important to appreciate the unique flavors of enlightenment in each tradition. For example, a Buddhist arahant's enlightenment is framed as insight into *emptiness and dependent origination*, whereas a Sufi saint's enlightenment is couched in the language of *divine love and union*. A Zen master might downplay conceptual descriptions entirely, pointing to a direct "here-now" experience, whereas a Hindu Vedantin might philosophically elaborate the identity of ātman and Brahman. These differences reflect rich cultural and philosophical contexts that have evolved around the enlightenment experience. Scholars have long debated whether all these traditions are describing the same ultimate experience in different guises (the "perennial philosophy" view), or whether the experiences themselves might have differing content because of doctrinal framing (Katz, 1984). While a definitive resolution to that debate lies beyond the scope of this report, the evidence surveyed suggests a convergence on key transformative elements. Such as the fall away of the individualistic mind and an encounter with what feels like an absolute reality (be it emptiness, God, or pure consciousness). As noted by philosopher David Loy (1982), there are deep parallels between Buddhist Nirvana and Hindu Moksha as liberative experiences, even if Buddhist non-theism and Hindu theism color the interpretation (Loy, 1982). Likewise, practitioners from different traditions often recognize each other's enlightenment. For instance, the Dalai Lama has spoken admiringly of Christian and Sufi mystics, and Hindu swamis have equated the Buddha's nirvāṇa with their own concept of samādhi – seeing a shared truth beyond names (Dalai Lama, 2005).

From an academic perspective, enlightenment remains a fascinating subject of interdisciplinary study, engaging theology, philosophy, psychology, and neuroscience. It challenges our understanding of the mind and its limits. The accounts assembled here, from Pāli canon scriptures and Upanishads to Rumi's poetry and modern memoirs, serve as data points mapping what William James called "states of consciousness of incomparable dignity." They invite us to consider that human development may extend into realms of insight and well-being far beyond the ordinary. At the same time, enlightenment is not portrayed as escapism or magical thinking; on the contrary, enlightened individuals are described as more in touch with reality, more present and effective in the world (albeit often in humble or unconventional ways).

In conclusion, spiritual enlightenment across traditions can be seen as the full flowering of human spiritual potential. It represents the discovery of our truest nature, whether defined as emptiness, spirit, God, or simply a natural mind free of delusion. This realization is universally accompanied by liberation from suffering and egocentrism and the emergence of boundless compassion. As the enlightened 8th-century Chinese Zen master Hui-Neng expressed in his *Platform Sutra*: *"Originally there is nothing (no fixed self); when we realize this, we behold our true nature, and suddenly we attain Buddhahood."* And as the enlightened Sufi poet Hafez sang: *"I am a hole in a flute that the Christ's breath moves through – listen to this music."* Both sentiments, though couched differently, capture the essence of enlightenment: the individual self becomes an empty vessel or a clear window, through which the light of the divine or the truth of reality can shine unobstructed. In every tradition, the enlightened person serves as an exemplary of what is possible for all, and inspiring others to undertake their own inward journey. The enduring message is one of hope: that beyond the tumult of the mind and the pains of the world, there is a state of consciousness that is peaceful, free, and whole, and it is attainable by those who earnestly seek it through whatever genuine path calls to them.

References

Boyce, B. (2006). Practicing the Great Perfection: Dzogchen Discussion. *Buddhadharma: The Practitioner's Quarterly*, Summer 2006. [Lion's Roar Magazine]. https://learning.tergar.org/wp-content/uploads/2020/08/Forum-Lions-Roar-Practicing-the-Great-Perfection.pdf

Böwering, G. (2016). Baqāʾ wa Fanāʾ. In *Encyclopaedia Iranica* (Vol. III, Fasc. 7, pp. 722–724). Retrieved from https://www.iranicaonline.org/articles/baqa-wa-fana-sufi-term-signifying-subsistence-and-passing-away/

Dalai Lama. (2005, November 12). Our faith in science [Op-ed]. The New York Times. Retrieved from https://www.dalailama.com/news/2005/our-faith-in-science

Dalai Lama. (2005). *The Universe in a Single Atom: The Convergence of Science and Spirituality*. Morgan Road Books.

Deutsch, E. (1969). Advaita Vedanta: A Philosophical Reconstruction. University of Hawaii Press. https://archive.org/details/advaitavedantaph0000deut/page/n5/mode/2up

Dimock, E. C., & van Buitenen, J. A. B. (2025). *Hinduism* (Karma, samsara, and moksha section). In *Encyclopaedia Britannica*. Retrieved August 2025, from https://www.britannica.com/topic/Hinduism

Easwaran, E. (2007). The Bhagavad Gita (2nd ed.). Tomales, CA: Nilgiri Press. https://openlibrary.org/books/OL8820230M/The_Bhagavad_Gita_(Classics_of_Indian_Spirituality)

Encyclopaedia Britannica. (n.d.). Satori (Zen Buddhism). Retrieved August 2025, from https://www.britannica.com/topic/Satori

Gethin, R. (1998). The Foundations of Buddhism. Oxford University Press. https://archive.org/details/foundationsofbud00rupe

Harvey, P. (2013). *An Introduction to Buddhism: Teachings, History and Practices: Second edition*. Cambridge University Press. https://assets.cambridge.org/97805218/59424/frontmatter/9780521859424_frontmatter.pdf

Holy Bible, New International Version. (2011). Zondervan. https://biblia.com/books/niv2011/offset/1176926

Idel, M. (2005). Kabbalah: New perspectives. Yale University Press.

Kapleau, P. (1989). The Three Pillars of Zen: Teaching, Practice, and Enlightenment. Anchor Books. https://archive.org/details/threepillarsofze0000kapl

Katz, S. (1984). Mysticism and Philosophical Analysis. Numen. https://doi.org/10.2307/3269957

Loy, D. R. (1982). Enlightenment in Buddhism and Advaita Vedanta: Are Nirvana and Moksha the Same? *International Philosophical Quarterly, 22*(1), 65–74. https://doi.org/10.5840/ipq19822217

Lutyens, M. (1971). *Krishnamurti: The Years of Awakening*. New York: Farrar, Straus and Giroux. https://archive.org/details/jkrishnamurtiyea0000luty

Keating, T. (1991). *Open mind, open heart*. Continuum. https://archive.org/details/openmindopenhear0000keat

Maharshi, R. (1985). Be As You Are: The Teachings of Sri Ramana Maharshi (D. Godman, Ed.). Penguin.

Martin, J. A. (2010). Extending the Continuum Model of Persistent Non-Symbolic Experiences in Adults. Journal of Consciousness Studies, 17(1–2), 111–125. https://nonsymbolic.org/PNSE-Article.pdf

McGinn, B. (2006). *The essential writings of Christian mysticism*. Modern Library. https://archive.org/details/essentialwriting0000unse_a0r0

Merton, T. (2003). *Contemplative prayer*. Orbis Books.

Nasr, S. H. (2009). The Garden of Truth ([edition unavailable]). HarperCollins. Retrieved from https://www.perlego.com/book/588853/the-garden-of-truth-pdf

PBS. (2005, November 18). *The Dalai Lama at the Aspen Institute*. Retrieved from https://www.pbs.org/wnet/religionandethics/2005/11/18/dalai-lama-aspen-institute/26747/

Rahula, W. (1959). *What the Buddha Taught*. New York: Grove Press. https://archive.org/details/BhanteWalpolaRahulaWhatTheBuddhaTaught

Radhakrishnan, S. (1953). The Principal Upanishads. London: George Allen & Unwin. https://archive.org/details/in.ernet.dli.2015.148291

Schimmel, A. (1975). Mystical Dimensions of Islam. University of North Carolina Press. https://archive.org/details/mysticaldimensionsofislam_201912

Scholem, G. (1995). *Major trends in Jewish mysticism*. Schocken Books. https://archive.org/details/scholem-gershom-gerhard-major-trends-in-jewish-mysticism_202308/page/n11/mode/2up

Sebastian, C. D. (2016). The cloud of nothingness. In *Sophia studies in cross-cultural philosophy of traditions and cultures*. https://doi.org/10.1007/978-81-322-3646-7

Siderits, M. (2023). *Buddha*. In E. N. Zalta & U. Nodelman (Eds.), *The Stanford Encyclopedia of Philosophy* (Spring 2023 Edition). Stanford, CA: Metaphysics Research Lab. Retrieved from https://plato.stanford.edu/entries/buddha/

Sivananda, Swami (n.d.). *Sri Ramana Maharshi*. In *Lives of Saints* [Web article]. Rishikesh, India: The Divine Life Society. Retrieved from https://www.dlshq.org/saints/sri-ramana-maharshi/

Smith, H. (1999). The World's Religions (Updated and revised ed.). HarperOne. https://archive.org/details/worldsreligionsp00hust

Suzuki, D. T. (1956). *Zen Buddhism: Selected Writings of D. T. Suzuki*. New York: Doubleday. https://archive.org/details/zenbuddhismselec00dais

Suzuki, S. (1970). ZEN MIND, BEGINNER'S MIND. In Trudy Dixon (Ed.), W E A T H E R H I L L (First edition). Weatherhill, Inc. https://www.holybooks.com/wp-content/uploads/Zen-Mind-Beginners-Mind-by-Shunryu-Suzuki.pdf

Taylor, S. (2017). The Leap: The Psychology of Spiritual Awakening. New World Library.

Tolle, E. (1999). *The Power of Now: A Guide to Spiritual Enlightenment*. Novato, CA: New World Library.

Underhill, E. (2002). *Mysticism: A study in the nature and development of spiritual consciousness*. Oneworld Publications. https://www.ccel.org/ccel/u/underhill/mysticism/cache/mysticism.pdf

Williams, P. (2008). Mahayana Buddhism. In *Routledge eBooks*. https://doi.org/10.4324/9780203428474

Wired. (2006, February 1). *Buddha on the Brain*. Retrieved from https://www.wired.com/2006/02/dalai

Wilber, K. (2000). *Integral Psychology: Consciousness, Spirit, Psychology, Therapy*. Boston: Shambhala. https://archive.org/details/integralpsycholo00wilb

Footnotes:

[1] Author and Citation Information for "Buddha"

https://plato.stanford.edu/cgi-bin/encyclopedia/archinfo.cgi?entry=buddha

[2] [9] Buddha (Stanford Encyclopedia of Philosophy)

https://plato.stanford.edu/entries/buddha/

[3] [4] [5] [6] [7] Cessation of Suffering

https://buddhist-world.com/four-realities/cessation-of-suffering/

[8] Enlightenment in Buddhism - Wikipedia

https://en.wikipedia.org/wiki/Enlightenment_in_Buddhism

[10] [11] [12] Hinduism - Karma, Samsara, Moksha | Britannica

https://www.britannica.com/topic/Hinduism/Karma-samsara-and-moksha

[13] Satori | Enlightenment, Awakening & Zen Philosophy | Britannica

https://www.britannica.com/topic/Satori

[14] [15] [16] [17] Forum: Practicing the Great Perfection | Lion's Roar

https://www.lionsroar.com/forum-practicing-the-great-perfection/

[18] [19] [20] [21] [22] [23] [24] BAQĀʾ WA FANĀʾ - Encyclopaedia Iranica

https://www.iranicaonline.org/articles/baqa-wa-fana-sufi-term-signifying-subsistence-and-passing-away/

[25] [26] Sri Ramana Maharshi – The Divine Life Society

https://www.dlshq.org/saints/sri-ramana-maharshi/

Appendices

Timeline for Belief Systems

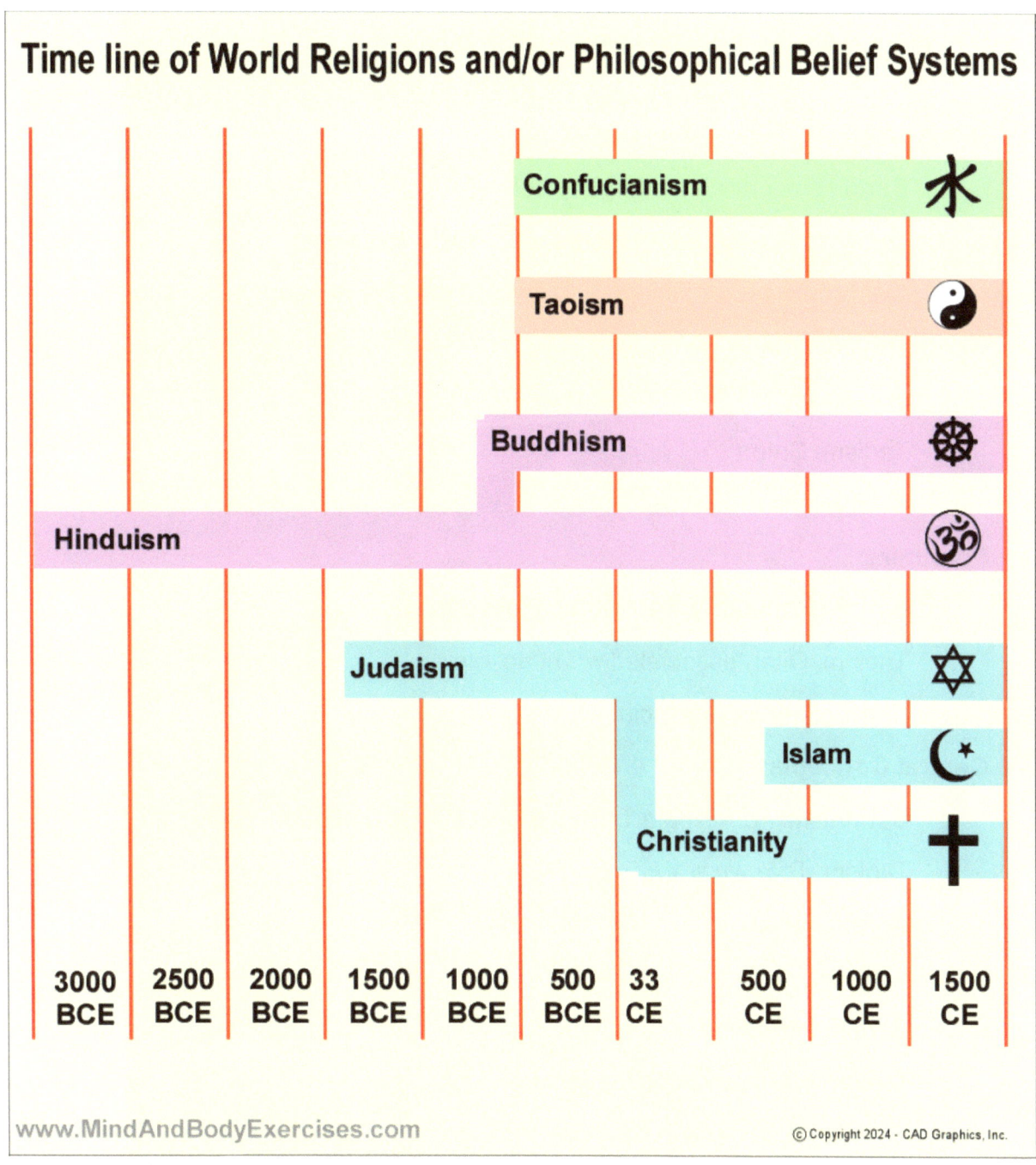

From my research, there is no historical evidence that supports that the founders of Buddhism (Siddhartha Gautama), Taoism (Lao Tzu), and Confucianism (Confucius) had ever met one another, crossed paths or had interactions during their lifetimes. All three of these individuals lived in different times and places. Based upon the geographical distances as well as cultural differences between them, it is quite unlikely that these founders could have shared any direct experience or even knowledge of each other's existence.

These traditions often share some of the same philosophical ideas. Similarities in philosophical topics cultivated by these systems are most likely due to common exploration of universal ethical and existential questions during their times, rather than direct interactions or encounters among the founders. These systems do also have unique differences in their goals, teachings, methods, traditions, and approaches to life.

Comparisons between the three systems:
- **Basic Goals:**
    - Buddhism: understanding the self.
    - Taoism: understanding the self in relation to all else.
    - Confucianism: understanding the self and the relationship to society.
- **Geographic Origins:**
    - Buddhism: India
    - Taoism: China
    - Confucianism: China
- **Founders:**
    - Buddhism: Siddhartha Gautama (Buddha)
    - Taoism: Often associated with Lao Tzu
    - Confucianism: Confucius
- **Central Concepts:**
    - Buddhism: Four Noble Truths, Eightfold Path, nirvana
    - Taoism: Tao, wu wei, yin & yang
    - Confucianism: Li, Jen, Te, Yi, Xiao
- **Ultimate Goal:**
    - Buddhism: Nirvana
    - Taoism: Harmony with the Tao
    - Confucianism: Social harmony through moral character and cultivation
- **Perspective on Life:**
    - Buddhism: reduce suffering, detach from desires.
    - Taoism: alignment and harmony with the Tao
    - Confucianism: ethical conduct and social responsibilities

Ancient Paths, Modern Peace: The Many Names of Enlightenment

In today's evolving conversation around holistic health, enlightenment is resurfacing-not just as an esoteric ideal, but as a practical and deep personal milestone within the journey toward total well-being. While often associated with mystics and monks, the essence of enlightenment has long been embedded across spiritual and philosophical traditions. It speaks to a universal longing: to understand oneself and one's place in the world, to live with clarity, and to experience inner peace.

Holistic health recognizes that true wellness includes not only the body but also the mind and spirit. When we explore enlightenment through this lens, it becomes less about dogma and more about the integration of awareness, connection, and personal transformation.

The Ancient Roots of Enlightenment: A Chronological Perspective

Across time and culture, humanity has reached for a transcendent state of wisdom and peace. Below is a historical look at how various traditions have been understood and named this experience:

1. Hinduism (c. 1500-1200 BCE)

Moksha refers to liberation from the cycle of rebirth (*samsara*) and the realization of one's oneness with the Absolute (*Brahman*). It emphasizes self-discipline, devotion, and philosophical inquiry-principles that resonate with today's holistic approaches to mindfulness and self-mastery.

2. Judaism (c. 1200-1000 BCE)

Devekut means "cleaving to God." It reflects an intense spiritual attachment and connection to the Divine, often nurtured through prayer, meditation on sacred texts, and acts of compassion. This mirrors modern interests in sacred ritual and spiritual intimacy within daily life.

3. Taoism (c. 600-400 BCE)

Wu Wei, or "effortless action," describes harmony with the *Tao*, or the natural order of the universe. It aligns beautifully with holistic living that promotes flow, simplicity, and balance through nature-based rhythms and minimalism.

4. Buddhism (c. 500 BCE)

Nirvana is the extinguishing of suffering, ignorance, and attachment. It is the ultimate liberation, discovered through the practice of mindfulness, ethical living, and meditative insight. *Bodhi*, or awakening, describes the experiential realization that leads to this state.

5. Christianity (c. 30 CE)

Illumination refers to the inner light that arises from divine communion. Practices like contemplative prayer, solitude, and service are paths to this inner radiance-echoing today's focus on stillness, presence, and soul care.

6. Islam (Sufism) (7th century CE)

Fana means the annihilation of the ego in the presence of God. In Sufi mysticism, it represents a deep surrender to divine love and truth-concepts that are increasingly embraced in emotional healing and ego work in holistic circles.

7. Sikhism (15th century CE)
Mukti signifies liberation from illusion and ego, and union with the Divine. It emphasizes selfless service, devotion, and equality principles foundational to both spiritual growth and community wellness.

8. New Age & Contemporary Spirituality (20th century CE onward)
Awakening / Self-Realization are the modern synthesis of East and West view of enlightenment as awakening to one's true nature. It often includes energy healing, intuitive development, and psychological integration-key aspects of the modern wellness movement.

Enlightenment and Holistic Wellness Today

In the context of holistic health, enlightenment is not about escaping the world. It's about engaging more deeply with it-intentionally, mindfully, and compassionately. Whether it's through yoga, mindful breathing, journaling, plant-based living, or spiritual inquiry, modern seekers are finding meaning in small, integrative practices that support mental clarity, emotional balance, and spiritual peace.

Importantly, enlightenment today is rarely seen as a final destination. Instead, it is a living process-a series of ongoing realizations and subtle shifts in consciousness. As individuals become more aware of their thoughts, behaviors, and purpose, they naturally align with states once reserved for sages and saints.

Why This Matters

In a time marked by information overload, stress, and disconnection, the timeless quest for enlightenment reminds us to return to our core. Holistic health is not just about the absence of disease-it is about the presence of meaning, clarity, compassion, and connection. Enlightenment, in all its cultural forms, is a call back to wholeness.

Whether you name it nirvana, moksha, awakening, or simply inner peace, the pursuit of higher awareness remains one of humanity's most enduring and necessary journeys.

Chamsa Meditation

Inner Vision, Pre-Birth Awareness, and the Mirror of Enlightenment

A Korean-Taoist Path of Self-Inquiry and Spiritual Return

Introduction

Within the quiet intersections of Korean martial arts, Seon Buddhism, Taoist inner alchemy, and indigenous contemplative practice, there exists a lesser-known meditative path called **Chamsa (참사)**. Translated loosely as "true reflection" or "sincere contemplation," this practice involves a series of inner visualizations that begin with the face and end with formless awareness. It guides the practitioner from physical identity, through spiritual regression, and into the vast, unconditioned presence that many traditions call enlightenment, *nirvana*, or union with the *Tao*.

Chamsa serves not only as a vehicle of personal transformation but also as a symbolic journey through layers of ego, memory, and form, toward a realization of the true self that was never born and never dies.

I. Origins and Conceptual Foundations

1. Linguistic Meaning

In Korean, **Cham (참)** means "true" or "authentic," while **Sa (사)** may refer to "thought," "contemplation," or "reflection" (Kim, 2018). Thus, Chamsa points to a practice of authentic inward reflection, aligned with the spiritual aim of uncovering the nature of self and reality.

2. Syncretic Influences

The practice bridges three major influences:

- ***Seon (Zen) Buddhism***: Emphasizes *hwadu* (Kōan-style inquiry), non-dual awareness, and meditation as a route to awakening (Aitken, 1990; Dumoulin, 2005).

- ***Taoist Neidan* (inner alchemy)**: Employs visualizations, energy return, and prenatal regression to restore original spirit (Komjathy, 2013; Yang, 1997).

- **Korean shamanic mysticism**: Embraces spiritual vision, ancestral awareness, and altered states as portals to insight (Kim, 2018).

II. The Stages of Chamsa Practice

Chamsa is typically taught as a stage-based meditation, though advanced practitioners may cycle through its phases in a single session. Each stage builds upon the last, guiding the practitioner from concrete visualization to subtle realization.

Stage 1: Face Visualization

- **Description**: Eyes closed, visualize your own face in full, accurate detail, every wrinkle, mole, and asymmetry. Include features such as the slope of the nose, eyebrow placement, asymmetries, scars, skin texture, color, and even the micro-expressions of your resting face. The image should be as vivid and lifelike as if one were looking into a mirror with eyes open.

- **Purpose**: Strengthen *shen* (spirit), develop internal focus, and anchor awareness in the "mind mirror." This aligns with Taoist inner vision practices (nèishì), projecting awareness from the third eye center or upper dantian (Kohn, 1993; Yang, 1997).

Stage 2: Dissolution of the Face

- **Description**: Allow the mental image of the face to gradually blur, dissolve, or melt away without force. Observe any resistance or attachment as the image fades.
- **Purpose**: Cultivate detachment from personal identity and begin breaking down the egoic image of the self. This mirrors both Zen and Taoist instructions for letting go of attachment to form (Dumoulin, 2005).

Stage 3: Witness Inquiry

- **Description**: With the face gone, turn awareness inward and ask: *"Who is seeing this image?"* or *"What remains when the face disappears?"*
- **Purpose**: This self-inquiry parallels Seon (Zen) Buddhism's hwadu method and Taoist "reflection on the void." It shifts attention to the formless witness, revealing the distinction between perception and identification (Aitken, 1990).

Stage 4: Womb Regression

- **Description**: Begin to visualize yourself in the womb. Sense the floating, fluid warmth of the pre-birth state. This visualization is not merely symbolic; it is a meditative immersion into pre-verbal, pre-identity awareness.
- **Purpose**: Return to the state of *yuan qi* and *yuan shen* (original energy and spirit), reconnecting with the undisturbed potential of consciousness prior to conditioning. This corresponds to Taoist embryonic breathing, and the process of returning to the origin (Komjathy, 2013).

Stage 5: Original Face

- **Description**: Let go of all visualizations. Abide in spacious presence. Ask: *"What was my original face before my parents were born?"*
- **Purpose**: This stage reflects the heart of Zen realization. All form, memory, and thought dissolve, revealing emptiness and unconditioned awareness (Aitken, 1990).

Stage 6: Return and Integration

- **Description**: Slowly bring awareness back to the breath, body, and senses. Open the eyes and re-engage with the outer world from this clarified state.

- **Purpose**: To integrate realization into daily life. The clarity cultivated through chamsa should inform one's behavior, relationships, and presence, aligning with both Taoist spontaneity and the Zen Ox-herding picture of reentering the world with open hands (Dumoulin, 2005; Yang, 1997).

Chamsa Meditation Progression

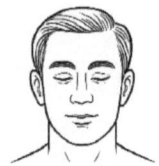  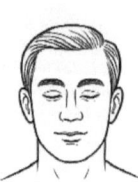 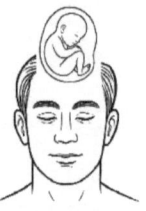 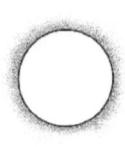 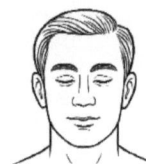

Face Visualization — Eyes closed, visualize your own face in full detail

Dissolution of the Face — Allow the face image to blur, dissolve, fade

Witness Inquiry — Ask, "Who is seeing this image?" or "Who am I?"

Womb Regression — Visualize within your mother's womb

Original Face — Ask, "What was your original face before your parents were born?"

Return & Integration — Gently return to your body and the external world

III. Practice Progression: Gradual vs. Cyclical

Progressive Practice (for most practitioners)

Stage	Timeframe	Developmental Aim
Face Visualization	1–2 weeks	Image clarity, stillness
Dissolution	1–2 weeks	Letting go, self-inquiry begins
Inquiry	2+ weeks	Direct experience of the observer
Womb Regression	Variable	Comfort with silence and non-conceptual being
Original Face	Ongoing	Insight into emptiness and non-duality

This mirrors the traditional model used in both Zen training and Taoist alchemical refinement (Komjathy, 2013; Dumoulin, 2005).

Cyclical Practice (for advanced practitioners)

Experienced meditators may move through all stages in a single sitting. This is often employed in advanced *neigong, zazen*, or during spiritual retreats (Yang, 1997).

IV. Chamsa and Enlightenment

1. As a Route to Enlightenment

Chamsa progressively dismantles the layers of self-identity. It leads to *direct realization* of formless presence, making it consistent with both Zen's gradual approach and Taoism's return to source (Aitken,1990; Komjathy, 2013).

2. As an Expression of Enlightenment

At deeper levels, the practice becomes a *reflection of the awakened state.* It is used not to attain enlightenment, but to maintain presence and live from insight (Dumoulin, 2005).

"The enlightened one returns to the marketplace with open hands." — Zen Ox-Herding Picture #10

V. Comparative Models of Enlightenment

Aspect	Chamsa	Zen Buddhism	Taoist Alchemy	Tibetan Dzogchen
Starting Point	Visualization of face	Hwadu or breath focus	Jing → Qi → Shen transmutation	Rigpa recognition
Key Turning Point	Dissolution and womb regression	"Great doubt" or koan resolution	Return to origin	Breakthrough to spontaneous presence
Final Aim	Witnessing the "original face"	Satori, then integration	Unity with Tao	Recognition of non-dual awareness
Method	Visual inquiry & regression	Self-inquiry & zazen	Breath, energy, visualization	Direct pointing-out instruction
Expression	Calm presence, embodied wisdom	Actionless action, compassion	Spontaneity, longevity, clarity	Effortless awareness, freedom

VI. Conclusion: Returning to the Formless Mirror

Chamsa meditation is both a method and a metaphor: a way of seeing the self by watching it dissolve. It begins with the familiar image of the face and guides the practitioner back to the unconditioned awareness before identity, thought, and time.

Whether used as a route to insight or a means of stabilization, Chamsa bridges Korean, Taoist, and Buddhist traditions. It reveals that the journey inward is not a retreat, but a return to that which has always been present.

"To know the self is to forget the self. To forget the self is to be enlightened by all things."
— Dōgen Zenji, *Genjōkōan*

References:

Aitken, R. (1990). *The Gateless Barrier: The Wu-Men Kuan (Mumonkan)*. North Point Press.
https://archive.org/details/gatelessbarrierw0000aitk

Dumoulin, H. (2005). *Zen Buddhism: A History (Vol. 2: Japan)*. World Wisdom. Zen Buddhism : a history : Dumoulin, Heinrich : Free Download, Borrow, and Streaming : Internet Archive

Kim, C. (2018). Korean shamanism. In *Routledge eBooks*.
https://doi.org/10.4324/9781315198156

Kohn, L. (1993). *The Taoist Experience: An Anthology*. SUNY Press.
https://archive.org/details/thetaoistexperienceliviakohn

Komjathy, L. (2013). *The Daoist Tradition: An Introduction*. Bloomsbury Academic.
https://www.bloomsbury.com/us/daoist-tradition-9781441168733/

Yang, J. (1997). *The Root of Chinese Qigong: Secrets of Health, Longevity, and Enlightenment*. YMAA.
https://archive.org/details/therootofchineseqigongbyyangjwingming1997

Be the Warrior, the Scholar, the Sage - a Blueprint to Happiness & Purpose

Jing (Essence)

Warrior Phase

Through practicing physical movements (Jing - essence), one can better develop:

1) Awareness – realization, perception or knowledge

2) Memory – the process of reproducing or recalling what has been learned or experienced

3) Coordination – bring actions together into a smooth concerted way

4) Control – skill in the use of restraint, direction and coordination

5) Endurance – ability to tolerate stress or hardship

6) Strength – power to resist or exert force

7) Stamina – combination of endurance and strength

8) Speed – rate of motion

9) Power – might or influence

10) Reflex – end result of reception, transmission and reaction

11) Strategy – a careful plan or method to achieve a goal

Mentally, these character traits are nurtured & refined:

Respect

Discipline

Self Esteem

Confidence

Determination to Achieve Goals

Qi (Energy)

Scholar Phase

Through practicing mental exercises (Qigong - vitality), one can better develop:

1) Relaxation of the muscles

2) Building of internal power

3) Strengthening of the organs

4) Improving the cardiopulmonary function

5) Strengthening the nerves

6) Improving vascular function

7) Can be practiced by the seriously ill

8) Help prevent injury to joints, ligaments & bones

9) Quicken recovery time from injuries & surgery

10) Building of athletic & martial arts power

11) Lessening of stress & balances emotions

12) Benefits sedentary individuals

Mentally, these concepts are comprehended & assimilated:

Human anatomy & physiology

Energy flow (Qi) with the energy meridians

Structural alignment of the skeletal & muscular systems

Shen (Spirit)

Sage Phase

Through practicing mediation exercises (Shen - consciousness), one can develop better understanding of:

1) The origin, nature, and character of things and beings

2) The human condition - study of human nature and conditions of life

3) The importance of communication on many different levels in order to share and disseminate wisdom

4) Sense of purpose

5) Making a difference

6) Self-less service to others

7) The inter-relationship between one another and how that can determine cause and effect

8) Our interaction between humans and the world (universe) we exist in

www.MindandBodyExercises.com

© Copyright 2023 - CAD Graphics, Inc.

About the Instructor, Author & Artist - Jim Moltzan

My fitness training started at the age of 16 and has continued for almost 45 years. During that time, I attended high school, then college, and worked 2 jobs all while pursuing further training in martial arts and other fitness methods. Many years ago, I started up an additional business to help finance my next goal of owning my own school. I moved to Florida from the Midwest to make this goal a reality. Having owned two wellness and martial arts schools, I have surpassed what I once believed to be my potential. At this stage in my life, I have chosen not to open any more schools, as I found the business aspects took too much focus away from my true passion: training and teaching others.

Beyond my professional endeavors, I am also a husband and father of two grown children. I believe that we must be prepared to work hard mentally, physically and financially to earn our good health and well-being. Not only for ourselves but for our families as well. Good health always comes at a cost whether in time, effort, cost, sacrifice or some combination of the previous.

I returned to college in my later 50's, to pursue my BS in Holistic Health (wellness and alternative medicine). My degree program covered many wide-ranging topics such as anatomy and physiology, meditation, massage, nutrition, herbology, chemistry, biology, history and basis of various medical modalities such as allopathic, Traditional Chinese Medicine, Ayurveda/yoga, naturopathy, chiropractic, and complimentary alternative methods. I also studied religion, mythology of the world, stress relief/management as well as sociology, psychology (human behavior) and cultural issues associated with better health and wellness.

Most of the movements I teach and write about originate from Chinese martial arts. The Qigong (breathing work) is from Chinese Kung Fu and the Korean Dong Han medical Qigong lineage. I have also gained much knowledge of Traditional Chinese Medicine (TCM) from many TCM practitioners, martial arts masters, teachers and peers. This includes many techniques and practices of acupressure (reflexology, auricular, Jing Well, etc.), acupuncture, moxibustion as well as preparation of some herbal remedies and extracts for conditioning and injuries. I have been studying for over 20 years with Zen Wellness, learning medical Qigong as well as other Eastern methods of fitness, philosophy and self-cultivation. I have been recognized as a "Gold Coin" master instructor having trained and taught others for at least 10000 hours or roughly over 35 years. The core fitness movements are from Kung Fu and its forms in Tai Chi, Baguazhang, Dao Yin and Ship Pal Gi (Korean Kung Fu and weapons training). Each martial art has mental, physical and spiritual aspects that can complement and enhance one another. The more ways that you can move your body and engage your mind, the better it is for your overall health.

Physical health, mental well-being and the relationships within our lives; are these the most cherished aspects of our existence? Yet, how much effort do we put towards improving these areas on a daily basis?

Many have used martial arts and other mind-body methods of training as methods of learning to see one's character as others see them. I feel that I can offer the priceless qualities of truth, honor and integrity with my instruction. You must seek the right teacher for you, because in time a student can become similar to their teacher. Through the training that I have experienced and offer to others, an individual can understand and hopefully reach their full potential.

By developing self-discipline to continuously execute and perfect sets of movements, an individual can start to understand not only how they work physically but also mentally and emotionally. You can find your strengths and your weaknesses and improve them both. Through disciplined training, one not only enhances physical abilities but also cultivates mental resilience, allowing them to achieve their fullest potential in all areas of life.

I have co-authored a book, produced numerous other books and journals, graphic charts and study guides related to the mind and body connection and how it relates to martial arts, fitness, and self-improvement. A few hundred of my classes and lectures are viewable on YouTube.com.

Lineage

- Recognized as a 1000 and 10,000-hour student and teacher
- Earned gold coins through the Doh Yi Masters and Zen Wellness program
- Earned a 5th degree in Korean Kung Fu through the Dong Han lineage

Education

Bachelor of Science in Holistic Medicine - Vermont State University

Books Available Through Amazon

https://www.amazon.com/author/jimmoltzan

Book Titles by Jim Moltzan

Book 1 - Alternative Exercises

Book 2 - Core Training

Book 3 - Strength Training

Book 4 - Combo of 1-3

Book 5 - Energizing Your Inner Strength

Book 6 - Methods to Achieve Better Wellness

Book 7 - Coaching & Instructor Training Guide

Book 8 - The 5 Elements & the Cycles of Change

Book 9 - Opening the 9 Gates & Filling 8 Vessels-Intro Set 1

Book 10 - Opening the 9 Gates & Filling 8 Vessels-sets 1 to 8

Book 11 - Meridians, Reflexology & Acupressure

Book 12 - Herbal Extracts, Dit Da Jow & Iron Palm Liniments

Book 13 - Deep Breathing Benefits for the Blood, Oxygen & Qi

Book 14 - Reflexology for Stroke Side Effects:

Book 15 - Iron Body & Iron Palm

Book 17 - Fascial Train Stretches & Chronic Pain Management

Book 18 - BaguaZhang

Book 19 - Tai Chi Fundamentals

Book 20 - Qigong (breath-work)

Book 21 - Wind & Water Make Fire

Book 22 - Back Pain Management

Book 23 - Journey Around the Sun-2nd Edition

Book 24 - Graphic Reference Book

Book 25 - Pulling Back the Curtain

Book 26 - Whole Health Wisdom: Navigating Holistic Wellness

Book 27 - The Wellness Chronicles (volume 1)

Book 28 - The Wellness Chronicles (volume 2)

Book 29 - The Wellness Chronicles (volume 3)

Book 30 - The Wellness Chronicles (complete edition, volumes 1-3)

Book 31 - Warrior, Scholar, Sage

Book 32 - The Wellness Chronicles (volume 4)

Book 33 - The Wellness Chronicles (volume 5)

Book 34 - Blindfolded Discipline

Book 35 - The Path of Integrity

Other Products

Laminated Charts 8.5" x 11" or 11" x 17" - over 200 various graphics (check the website)

Qigong - Chi Kung
SKU: ChiKung

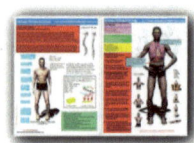

The human body is made up of bones, muscles, and organs amongst other components. Veins, arteries and capillaries carry blood and nutrients throughout to all of the systems and components. Additionally, 12 major energy medians carry the body's energy, "life force" also known as "chi". Ones chi is stored in the lower Dan Tien. Daily emotional imbalances accumulate tension and stress gradually affecting all of the body's systems. Each discomfort, nuisance, irritation or grudge continues to tighten and squeeze the flow of the life force. This is where "dis-ease" claims its foothold.

Strengthen Your Back (set #1)
SKU: StrengthenYourBack1

Good health of the lower back starts with good posture. The following set of exercises develop strength and flexibility which improve posture. Strength in the back, hips and abdominals provide a strong cage that houses the internal organs. Flexibility in these areas helps to maintain good blood circulation to the organs and lower body. Lengthening of the spine while exercising reduces stress and tension on the nervous system.

Broadsword 1-10
SKU: Broadsword

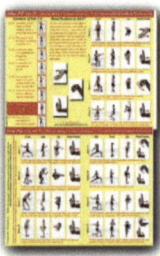

Broadsword training develops the body, mind and spirit well beyond that which can gained from empty hand training alone. The Broadsword has many different sets to be mastered utilizing quick, fluid and precise movements.

Ship Pal Gye set 7 (Kung Fu stance training)
SKU: ShipPalGye7

SHIP PAL GYE or Ship Par Gay, is a Korean version of Chinese Shaolin Lohan Qigong, meaning "18 chi movements" or what were supposedly the original 18 drills that Bodhidharma introduced to the Shaolin monks. It is reputed to be the basis for the Shaolin Kung Fu, which in turn, greatly influenced the developments of all branches of Asian fighting arts.

Noble Stances
SKU: NobleStances

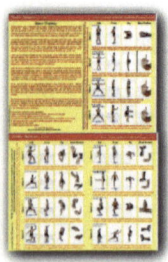

Noble stances are a combination of various stances from different styles of Chinese martial arts. Stances, in this case, meaning correct placement of the feet, knees, hips, and arm positions relative to ones center of gravity. Executing static positions and holding the particular body positions for anyway from a few seconds to several minutes reaps many benefits foremost being able to cultivate a strong and healthy core.

Contacts

For more information regarding charts, products, classes and instruction:

www.MindAndBodyExercises.com
info@MindAndBodyExercises.com

www.youtube.com/c/MindandBodyExercises
www.MindAndBodyExercises.wordpress.com

407-234-0119

Social Media:

Facebook: MindAndBodyExercises
Instagram: MindAndBodyExercises
Twitter: MindAndBodyExercise

Jim Moltzan - Mind and Body Exercises
522 Hunt Club Blvd. #305
Apopka, FL 32703

Website

Blog

YouTube Channel

www.ingramcontent.com/pod-product-compliance
Lightning Source LLC
Chambersburg PA
CBHW042004150426
43194CB00002B/117